# 5 rules of
# operative
# optimization

Marcus Karl HAMAN, MSc

production management for managers

An employee cannot be motivated; however, an environment can be created, wherein the employee motivates himself.

*Marcus Karl Haman*

# 5 rules of operative optimization

production management for managers

Bibliographical information of the German National Library:

The German National Library registers this publication in the German National Bibliography, detailed bibliographical data internet, which can be available over http://dnb.dnb.de.

Illustration: **Marcus Karl HAMAN, MSc,**

**canstockphoto.at**

Further participants **HCA-consulting GmbH**
Translation: Chitale Prakash

Production and Published by: BoD– Books on Demand, Norderstedt

ISBN: 9783752684414

# Inhaltsverzeichnis

## INTRODUCTION

Especially in the crisis period it is observed again and again that undertakings, which rested in the sunshine of positive order position, they face in crisis period the icy frost of the market. Orders break away, or are at least reduced and thus also the profits, which ensured the carefree business life in the comfort zone. Less orders and, less contribution margins inevitably produce in-house pressure to act. The negative spiral begins to rotate and before one makes a mistake, the slowly rotating negative spiral becomes a turbo and it appears, as if this could not be stopped any more. The fixed costs eat up the iron reserves of the company in the shortest possible period, and if then massive countermeasures are not implemented, follows that thing, which no businessman likes to see, namely the insolvency.

This can be counteracted in time with corresponding measures in the finance area as also in operative field of action of the core business. Preventively as also during the crisis, operative optimizations are possible and helpful, when it is necessary to make the undertaking better or more resistant to the market slumps.

And one thing in advance – Sitting out a crisis, this can be done by the least number of units and organizations. The reason for this lies in the fixed costs, which cannot be so quickly modified or adjusted. An undertaking in the productive environment can use 3 screws, in order to influence the operative costs positively. To keep the stocks as low as possible, to increase the productivity or the throughput, and to reduce the operating costs. In order to reduce the operating costs a little more analysis is required. Here the competence onion helps to illustrate all relevant and not so significant competences and processes. Processes cause costs as well as resources (employees). It should be considered as to which processes and competences are really required in an undertaking. Fixed costs influence the Cash Flow, i.e. the liquidity of the organization and during demanding times every Euro should be considered, much more than during the normal business period.

From several years of experience in business life it can determined that a number of undertakings can post very restricted reserves (Cash) and the survival of the unit assumes a critical status after 2-3 months of „LOCKDOWN".

The knowledge from several assignments as Interim Manager, also called manager for a period, or also addressed as industrial mercenary, is, that it requires rules to implement successful modifications. Not as a template but much rather as guide in order to find again and again to find the right path. Because what should be achieved lies on the hand.

It is necessary to do the RIGHT things and to do the things RIGHTLY!

# 5 RULES OF OPERATIVE OPTIMIZATION

To define the rules is one thing, to implement the rules is quite a different challenge, especially since the entire organization must be involved and must be „fetched" for the improvement trip. The inclusion of all the employees is the most important of all the pre-requisites, followed by standards, the conversion of quality measures, short run/implementation and decision-making periods and not to forget implementation of continuous consequence -measures and to continuously develop the organization further. If the organization considers and ensures these conditions on a very broad basis, then the first important step is taken, and the 5 rules can be employed successfully with high probability.

The 5 rules of the operative optimization are not a rocket science and certainly do not require any special training, although a basic prerequisite must be brought in by the respective organization and this without the "if" and "but" – namely the will for change.

The 5 rules of the operative optimization are the following:

1. Find the core competence
2. Implement transparent key figures
3. Control loops are your friends
4. Remove complexity
5. Define roles & responsibilities

# FIND THE CORE COMPETENCE

Every undertaking has a core competence. This raises a claim, since in the core competence also the profit is generated, to be able to stand on the background of the attention of the entire organization.

Many undertakings believe to be able to demonstrate several core competences and thus commit a substantial error. Several core competences mean multi-front wars in the hotly contested market and multi-front wars, as history teaches us, were crowned with success in the most seldom cases. The reason lies in the division of the existing resources and knowledge carriers on the individual topics.

Comparable in an example, with 2 different approaches of restaurants.

Restaurant Number 1:
The menu endlessly long and a lot of foods from very different countries, from Asiatic to French cuisine up to Italian gourmet food and everything from one and the same kitchen.

Restaurant Number 2:
The daily menu very small and manageable, with materials purchased fresh from the

market and finely prepared in the kitchen. Specializes itself to the regional kitchen.

Restaurant1, with several core competences in the form of foods from different countries.

Restaurant2, with only one core competence and a daily menu of the regional kitchen.

And now the quiz question:
Where shall the taste be better?

To be able to offer everything and to control the market with that is a misconception.
Sometimes the argument is made that AMAZON indeed sells everything. From the underwear up to the parquet floor. That is true, however AMAZON does not have a core competence in the manufacture of these goods but rather in the sale of the same and in that, AMAZON is really good.
And similar is the pattern in other industries. An unending number of competences cannot be developed without there being a loss of quality. And it is the quality, which the long-term customer relations ensure and thus minimize the risk of not surviving in the market.

## THE COMPETENCE ONION

How does an organization find its core competence and what distinguishes a competence from a core competence?

The difference between a competence and a core competence is that with the core competence the profit is generated and there the knowledge and the capability of the organization is very pronounced. Further competences can also be present in an undertaking; however, they do not depict the main business. Much rather the further competences can be found in the supporting areas.

When all the competences are considered, then a distinction can be made between core competences and support competences.

A further classification of the supporting competences lies in the „necessary" competences, which the core competence supports actively and competences, which are also available in the undertaking, however are independent from the core competence.

Thus, when graphically represented, a kind of onion is formed. The core is formed by the core competence, and the further away from the core, the lesser is the relevance of other competences for the core business, or for the core competence.

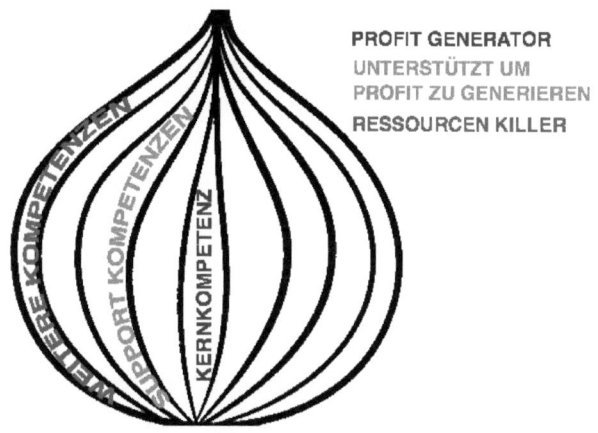

PROFIT GENERATOR
UNTERSTÜTZT UM
PROFIT ZU GENERIEREN
RESSOURCEN KILLER

The core competence also identifies the core process. Thus, the competences are to be equated with the processes. Core processes indicate the profit-generating processes, whereby except for the supporting processes, all the further processes can also be seen as resource killer.

QUESTIONING IS PERMITTED!

Also, when in many undertakings the questioning of individual processes and competences by own employees is not liked very much, the top management itself should allow once the objecting and questioning. Managers, who would like to be measured on the number of employees, for whom they are responsible, it must be clearly said that it is the profit which must be increased and not the number of employees, even when it sounds very sexy in the reputation circle of the manager to be shown as responsible for thousands of employees. Employees mean costs, which cannot be so easily adjusted, when it is not running so well. Managers should rather refer to that, as to how much profit could be generated with which deployment.

The questioning and classification of the individual components and processes in to the three earlier described categories

- Core process
- Supporting processes &
- All other existing processes

is essential and should be repeatedly

subjected to a validity test, in order to save costs in a sensible manner.

It must be the objective to reduce to an absolute minimum the third category „other available processes/competences "or to outsource them. These are „Resource killers" and they cause only headaches in most of the cases.

Concentration and total focus on processes and competences, which generate profit.

In every process there are problems which appear now and then or regularly. Problems are challenges, which must be solved in order to place the undertaking better in the market. The solving of the problems brings the undertaking further – in many fields and subjects. The history behaves differently, when it deals with the third category of processes. There are problems which only cause costs and during the solution of the problem do not bring any additional value for the organization. Resources, which could be deployed better, must solve problems, which only have conditional influence on the business profit. These expenses can be considered as wastage and should be stopped as quickly as possible. For every service there is at least one undertaking, which has specialized in it and sees the core competence in this service. These undertakings have aligned their total organization to this core competence, and they are mostly more efficient in this subject than the own organization.

## A CASE STUDY

As example a wage production for metal punching parts (sheet metal area)

The core competence lies in the fabrication of metallic punched parts as per client specifications. Like many undertakings, this undertaking has also grown in the course of time and manages itself all the departments in the undertaking. After a sighting/analysis of the existing competences and processes, the processes and competences were subdivided in the following groups.

**Core Competence:**

- Punching of metal parts as per customer requirements

**The supporting competences are the following:**

- Tool maintenance
- Service & maintenance of punching machines
- Quality management & quality assurance
- Internal adjustment logistic, Packing & Despatch

**Further Competences:**

- Safety specialist & environment
- Purchase
- Logistics
- IT
- Personnel billing
- Legal
- Bookkeeping
- Controlling
- Tax law
- Etc.

During an analysis period it could be determined that many problems and the greatest resource possibilities for removing the problems were not to be found in the core process.

From the knowledge, measures should be worked out for improvement. In order to carry this out the organization requires transparent and clearly defined characteristic numbers, so called KPIs. From gut feeling action should be taken in the least number of cases. Also, the over-perfectionist style is to be questioned, since the decision-makers are found in micro-management and thus are lost in detail, instead of remaining on the flight path, which it needs in order not to lose the overall picture from the "eyes". The courage for gap is also necessary here in order to act effectively in an efficient and controlled manner.

The courage for gap

DER MUT ZUR LÜCKE

## QUESTIONNAIRE:

- How do the 5 rules of operative optimization sound?

- What is a core competence?

- How do I find the core competence?

- What does the competence onion state?

- What does one understand under the concept „The courage for gap?"

## IMPLEMENT TRANSPARENT KEY FIGURES!

Key figures show the way. With this device the decision maker is well advised. Only as defined, or if the manager finds the right operative key figures. In many undertakings, in the course of time, the so-called numerical cemeteries have appeared, which were never subjected to a validity check. And thus, these resource killers' slumber and multiply themselves partly through the addition of new key figures and cause costs, due to the required attention by the employees. And let us be to the point, this is pure wastage.

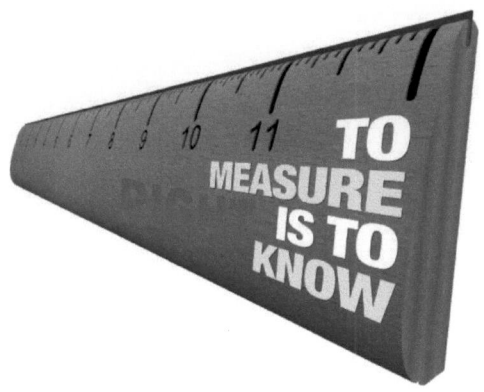

A failure recipe is certainly not to retire these key figures; however, this lies often in the fear of the management to make the corresponding decision to retire these.

With the attitude not to question the existing circumstances and not to take the corresponding decisions, or not to implement them, the organization becomes more and more lame and inactive

## CLEARING OF KEY FIGURES / LESS IS MORE!

There should be culture in the undertaking, question key figures once in a year and to subject them to a validity check. It pays, when one considers the possibility of savings, which result due to this much more easily. Number cemeteries deserve to be occupied with resources, even though no one sees them. They are worked out, processed and perhaps represented in a presentation, which an employee creates in tedious work.

However, what makes a right key figure, also called KPI – (Key Performance Indicator)? A meaningful key figure enables a control of the organization. On operating basis in a production undertaking it is certainly the key figure „UP-TIME". Uptime contains the technically available working period of a plant, machine, etc. The higher this number is, specified in %, the more efficiently the plant/machine etc. produces. In the theoretical case, up to 100%. And therefore, in the theoretical case, because there are always disturbance factors. Whether it be due to a planned or unplanned standstill, as for instance a tool change or a conversion process, cleaning process, an electrical disturbance etc. The possibilities in this regard are manifold. Since the statement of this key figure impairs the profitability, this is to be seen as very relevant. As against this is perhaps a key figure, as to how many empty boxes stand in the yard, not so important, since these containers are perhaps not used any more. Only that should be measured, what impairs success.

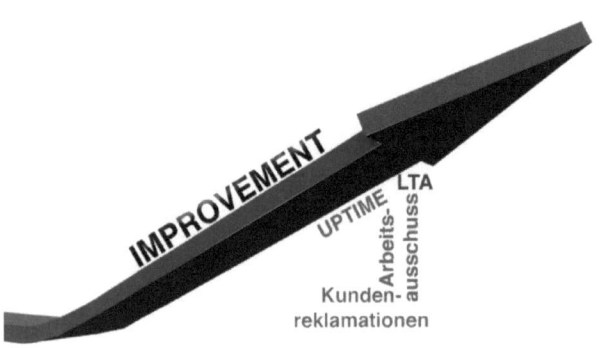

Essentially there are only 3 questions which should be asked:

- Can the undertaking be more profitable through the key figure, or does the key figure show the way to success?

- Does the key figure help to ensure continuous improvements, or?

- Is the key figure a resources killer?

To question key figures regularly in annual rhythm pays off by becoming „slimmer".

## KEY FIGURE DEFINITION BRINGS CLARITY

It is generally valid – each key figure must be clearly defined. The reason for this lies in the reproducing ability of the key figure. If no knowledge of the compilation is available, what is the key figure now worth?

A definition brings understanding and meaningfulness into every key figure. This becomes very clear in the key figure OEE (**O**verall **E**quipment **E**ffectiveness). This key figure is not standardized; thus, this key figure is calculated in different ways. Also, within an organization, there can be different interpretations, should the key figure not have been clearly defined.

Thus comparability and „Benchmarking" become impossible.

KEY FIGURE DEFINITION OEE (example)
Distribute to: all Locations

## 1.Purpose

Definition of the operative KPI – Key figures (Shop-floor Management), designation, unit, type of calculation and for representation on KPI overview sheet. Hanging at respective TIC – Team Info Center

## 2.Scope

Production area

## 3. Availability

Formula for the availability

$$Availability = \frac{\text{Actual Production time (actual) of OK parts in minutes}}{\text{Possible production time (Target)}}$$

Possible production time = actual production time (OK parts production time) + unplanned downtime time in minutes

Calculation of availability

Possible production time (TARGET):
One shift takes always 8 hours. Converted in minutes this gives:

8 hours x 60 minutes = 480 minutes.

480 minutes is thus the maximum time (Target time) which a machine can run in one shift.

Planned downtime periods are to be deducted from the possible TARGET time for instance from 480 minutes per shift.

Planned downtime periods are:

- Planned maintenance and repair assignments
- Planned Trainings
- Non-scheduled time of the plant (Planning)
- Pauses (when the plant requires a cycle-related employee and when no production is possible during the pause

Short term repairs and unplanned downtime /obstructions of any kind should not be deducted.

Reason:

Only that time should be shown as possible production time, which can be really allocated to production. Unplanned periods of planning (no order) would deteriorate the result of production, without the production having an influence. Polluter principle.

The key figure accessibility should reflect the efficient use of the plants by production. Therefore, it is important not to project all the sales themes here.

*ATTENTION: On the day of the time difference these are exceptionally 7 or 9 hours.*

The actual production period represents the real time, in which the machine has produced as per plan and produced OK components/products. Exclusive unplanned downtime are:

## Unplanned downtimes:

Unplanned downtime are periods, in which the plant/machine stands still and does not produce.

- Faults of the plant/machine
- Absence of employee due to sickness etc.
- Missing Material
- Absence of fabrication order – not as per Plan
- Waiting for maintenance
- Waiting for quality approvals
- Power failure
- Etc

## Output:

Formula for the output:

$$\text{Output} = \frac{\text{ACTUAL output (in m / in min)} \quad \text{ONLY OK METER}}{\text{EXPECTED output (in m / in min)}}$$

Calculation of the output

ACTUAL Output (in m & in min.):

GOOD products (OK products) per minute, reflects the produced good products in minutes, which were manufactured in a period X (Calculation period).

Calculation period = Shift or day or week or month

The calculation period, both for numerator as well as denominator.

ACTUAL output (in m & in min.):

EXPECTED output is the possible number of meters, which could have been produced in the calculation period.

Quality:

Formula for the Quality

$$Quality = \frac{\Sigma \text{ produced parts} - \Sigma \text{ reworked parts} - \Sigma \text{ Rejected parts}}{\Sigma \text{ all produced parts}}$$

## Calculation of the Quality

Both the numerator as well as the denominator of the formula must be in the same unit.

## 4. Calculation OEE

Formula for the OEE:

OEE = Availability X Output X Quality

Overview for the OEE:

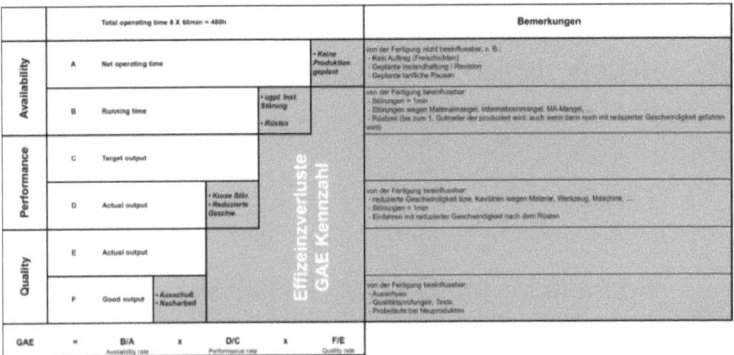

## 5.Procedure

Calculation of the OEE as per Formula Entry

in KPI overview sheet on monthly basis

## 6.Calculation

OEE = Availability X Output X Quality

## 7.Reporting

Responsible: Manager Production
Frequency: monthly
KPI-overview sheet shows:
monthly value in % of plant utilization
Target: is shown on the KPI – overview sheet
of the respective year

## 8.Simultaneously valid documents

KPI – Overview sheet
KPI – Grafic P – OEE

## 9.Change vis a vis the last Version

Version 1.0

| prepared, ~~changed~~ | geprüft | freigegeben |
|---|---|---|
| Name:M. HAMAN | Name: | Name: |
| Date: 20.12.20 Ver.:1.0 | Date: | Date: |

## OPERATIVE KEY FIGURES ARE NO SECRETS!

One of the absolutely basic rules in optimization is the inclusion of all employees. During the continuous improvement this rule is the key to success. Key figures show the way, however, when no one knows the key figure or understands it, then, as good as it may be, it is to be considered as „senseless".

An improvement is implemented profitably only on a broad base, since otherwise there is no sustainability. And without sustainability there is no success, which can also be measured, or which can also be visible in the P&L (profit and loss account).

Therefore, the relevant key figures should be published on team boards or factory boards, which are freely accessible to all the employees. Only so all the employees can follow the success or failure and apply themselves correspondingly motivated. Not knowing where the undertaking stands and where the problems lie, does not promote the motivation to change something or to go the extra mile. However, when the employees see the key figures and understand them, they recognize the necessity to work on them actively or to bring themselves in it.

An employee cannot be motivated; however,

an environment can be created, wherein the employee motivates himself

A good preparation and the implementation of a standard for all boards, which is self-explanatory, would be very helpful and very much to be recommended. The employee must rediscover himself in the key figures. There is no sense to hang out key figures, which cannot influence the employees or which they do not understand. Only when the employees recognize their contribution, success shall not be wanting.

Operative key figures in the following columns can help to strengthen the understanding with respect to many measures. For the sake of simplicity, it is recommended to make an effort for a structure of clarity.

The team or factory board should be constructed on 2 axes. The vertical axis with the PDCA control circuit and the horizontal axis with the individual rubrics.

The individual columns are:

- Work safety & environment
- Quality
- Productivity
- Costs
- Stocks
- Organization development

The allocation should be carried out to the abovementioned areas and provided with key figures, where the employees rediscover themselves and with their activities, with their cooperation to carry out an active part of the implementation.

The PDCA control circuit, which is executed on the vertical axis, controls the individual stages of the key figures.

Point P, PLAN, the superior objectives, which are designed for long term, are communicated.

Point D, DO or to do, shows the corresponding graphic for the key figure.

Point C, CHECK–SCRUTINIZE, shows in simple form with the traffic light colors, which status the key figure shows.

Point A, ACT – ACT, describes in measure sheets the countermeasures, which shall hit in case of deviation from the target.

A schematic representation of a Team Board could look as follows:

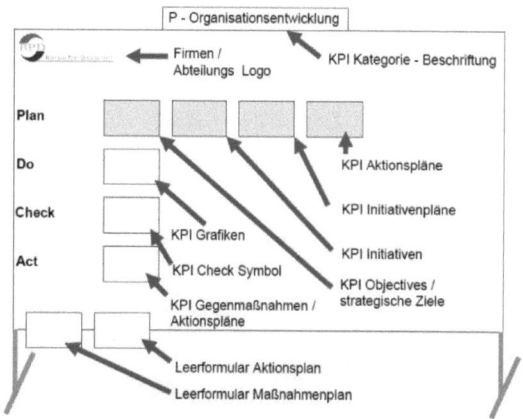

## KEY FIGURES SHOW THE WAY

With the „unraveled", the clearly defined key figures and the visual representation on a board, a way to success is shown. How? Quite simple, during the observation of the meaningful figures it can be recognized, in which key areas there is a need for action to introduce measures and to process them consistently. Provided that targets were also set for every key figure or agreed upon. Should this not be the case, then it is rewarding to call in memory the previously described 3 set screws.

The three set screws of a productive organization are:

1. Reduce stocks
2. Increase Productivity / throughput &
3. Reduce operating costs

Und at least these 3 targets are to be followed and to be followed with measures, even though these 3 set screws represent superior objectives. To be broken down here would be the next step.

An example should show this as illustration:

An example to reduce the operating costs would be the analysis of the work accidents and injuries. When this key figure does not show 0, then it is definitely necessary here to work out measures. Why in case of work accidents? What do work accidents have to do with operating costs?

The answer lies in the absentees of the employees caused by work accidents. Absentees, which must be compensated by other employees, and this causes costs in personnel, or a reduction of performance, since other employees experience a clear additional stress.

Another example is the quality fault costs. Every fault on the product causes costs. And the nearer the faulty part comes to the customer, the higher are the costs for this. Countermeasures, so that this fault can never come again, would be a sustainable solution and they lead inevitably to cost savings.

If the faults on a plant are reduced, this influences the key figure UPTIME positively and a higher production would be the consequence.

In other words, more OK products are manufactured and thus they reduce the cost share of each individual product of the undertaking, so that with the same number of employees a higher spreading could be achieved.

A large number of examples of this can be counted here.

If the organization orients itself to the 3 set screws of production, even without agreed upon targets, the right measures can be implemented in order to save costs in a sensible manner.

## QUESTIONNAIRE:

- Why do key figures show the way?

- What are KPIs?

- How does a KPI key figure distinguish itself from other key figures?

- What is a key figure cemetery?

- Why do key figures show the way?

- How is a key figure defined?

## CONTROL CIRCUITS ARE YOUR FRIENDS

In order to ensure a continuous progress of improvement, control circuits are essential. However, control circuits are only then effective, when they possess the following characteristics:

- No large number of participants
- Clear structure and process
- Communication of the expectations of the discussion
- All participants know the process or the questionnaire
- All participants are punctual and prepared
- The control circuit is not a problem-solving round
- Each participant takes over the responsibility for his area and measures
- Measures are recorded in the measure plans and provided with deadlines and responsibilities.
- There can always be only one responsible person for one point of the measures
- The control circuit reacts on factual

basis and is not a „Finger- pointing" / fault finding exercise

Control circuits, as the name already says, take place regularly. The purpose is that problems are documented and presented, or the persons responsible for the individual measures remain on the subjects, till these were sustainably implemented.

Like many systems, the control circuits have two pages. On one page the team receives many measures for implementation. In many instances, an additional load is the consequence. On the other hand, the team also receives decisions and support from the top management, because this can withdraw itself equally less from the responsibility, as the employees on the line. Thus, many pending topics are finally rightly addressed and a decision, in the one or the other direction, is the consequence of the same. Thus, the organization moves in the right direction on the stony path to success. Prerequisite for this is the consistent procedure and implementation.

An example of a control circuit:

The morning meeting on shopfloor

The morning meeting on shopfloor takes place near the Team Info Board, where the key figures are hanging.

The participants are from the responsibility areas. The questionnaire is always constant, and it is queried by the person with overall responsibility.

Since these are always the same questions, no participant can use the excuse, he had not known what was expected from him.

The daily meeting process looks as follows:

**DAILY MEETING**

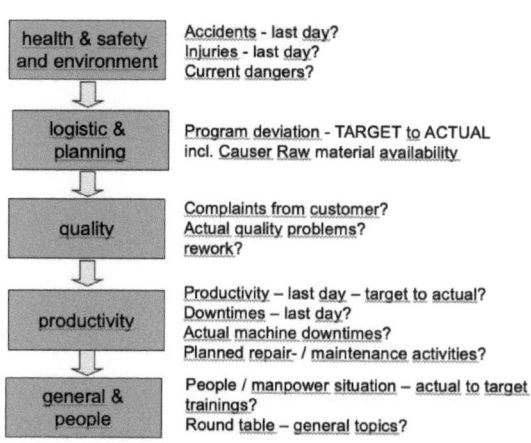

| | |
|---|---|
| health & safety and environment | Accidents - last day?<br>Injuries - last day?<br>Current dangers? |
| logistic & planning | Program deviation - TARGET to ACTUAL incl. Causer Raw material availability |
| quality | Complaints from customer?<br>Actual quality problems?<br>rework? |
| productivity | Productivity – last day – target to actual?<br>Downtimes - last day?<br>Actual machine downtimes?<br>Planned repair- / maintenance activities? |
| general & people | People / manpower situation – actual to target trainings?<br>Round table – general topics? |

It must be said clearly here that the work safety affects everyone to some extent, and everyone is responsible for it, however, only one person can be responsible for the points in the totality.

The „ROUND" table under the section "general & people", gives every participant the possibility to refer to general points. It should be remembered that this discussion as a rule does not last longer than approx.
15 minutes. However, at the beginning it can also become an hour, since not all processes

have become familiar.

Through the control circuits key figures are referred to with measures and continuously attended or effectively followed up.

## DEFINE VALUABLE DISCUSSIONS

In many undertakings there are numerous discussions. Many of those have originated before a long period and have perhaps no claim to be continued or no justification to survive any more. However, these key figure cemeteries are equally less questioned. How many managers waste time in senseless discussions, which do not represent any extra value for the undertaking? How much time could be gained for the managers, when unnecessary discussions are simply avoided? Organizations must themselves answer these questions, from experience it can however be said that as a rule these are too many. As to where these discussions take place is also a subject by itself.

A discussion which takes place regularly and which has the purpose to influence the core business, the production, positively, due to following reasons, takes place also at the location of the happening.

- The key figure boards can be referred to
- The discussion takes place in standing position at a round table
- The employees on the Shopfloor see that the management takes interest in their problems
- The employees can read at any time the results and planned measures on board
- etc

## DEFINE YOUR CONTROL CIRCUITS

Which control circuits are worthy to be implemented? What does the organization need in order to ensure a continuous improvement? Because, it is the declared objective, to transfer the organization to a learning organization.

Control circuits are discussions on a „regular" basis, with specific focus on the core competence. In our case study the production, which considers the fabrication of parts as core process and also generates the profit with that.

As recommendation the following control circuits would have to be implemented:

**Daily Discussions:**

- daily discussion

The daily discussion means to discuss the previous and the current working day.

## Weekly Discussions:

- Quality discussion
- Performance or output discussion
- Eventually team meeting

During the quality discussion all the relevant topics of the previous week and the current week are discussed. Also, during the Performance Meeting, where the provided performance, called UPTIME, stands in focus. In the team meetings all the aspirations of the team, as well as trainings and instructions are implemented.

**Monthly Discussions:**

- Business Plan Deployment Review

The Business Plan Deployment Meeting has the objective to discuss all operative key figures over the last month in the areas of work safety & environment, quality, productivity costs, stocks and organization development and in case of deviations from the objective to check the countermeasures and if required, to pass further measures.

**Quarterly Discussions:**

- Work Safety Committee

Additional discussions like KVPs or project discussions should be carried out without influence, however, not as control circuit.

It is important, and this cannot be mentioned often enough, that clear sequences of the individual discussions, inclusive of a questionnaire should be defined and the employees should be trained for these.

## MANAGEMENT ON SITE

Good as the control circuits are, without the presence of the management it is only half the thing. And with this we come to quite a sensitive topic of the culture of the undertaking.

Culture is always lived from the top and it must be exemplified, without compromises!

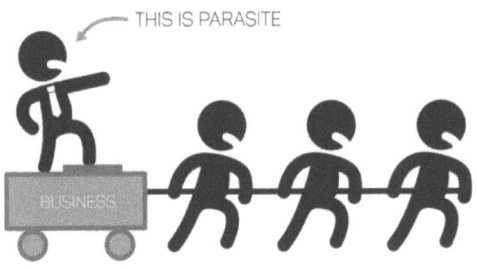

Without the clear „commitment" of the top management it would not come consistently to the employee, and especially the most sensitive level, the middle management becomes rather restrained without the involvement and clear statement of the top management, if not acting in a partially blocking manner. And thus, a consistency, which is so important, is not present. However, it needs more than a mere statement from the top. Here the engagement through presence on the shopfloor is equally essential, like the active support and acceptance of responsibility. On the production level there are demands for decisions, which cannot be made by the team. Here it is important to catch the „Ball" and to show clearly that the Top Management is part of the team and the solution. The decisions on the short decision track shows in clear language that the problems and topics on the shopfloor are important for the undertaking. Because the top management must always have one thing before its eyes:

The undertaking exists for one single reason – to generate profits. And the profit always comes to a great extent from the core competence of the undertaking.

In the ideal instance a manager should assume a leader's role, also called, LEADER Role in modern German. Thus, he automatically becomes a team member and sees himself as part of the team provided with a different role and responsibility.

## QUESTIONNAIRE:

- What are control circuits?

- Why are control circuits so important?

- What influence does the management have on the performance of the undertaking?

- What is meant by Management on site?

- What is the difference between Manager and Leader?

## REMOVE COMPLEXITY

By nature, man is a hunter and collector. The manager of today is not spared from this. This can be experienced in many undertakings in the form of preserving actions and decisions. Support processes are not questioned, existing processes are retained, since no risk is taken in order not to activate wrong decisions and god forbid, to have to accept the responsibility for that as well. So long as the undertaking makes profits, in many instances with great liking the path of least resistance is taken. Why put yourself in danger, when the shop is running? Now, the answer is obvious:

After the crisis is before the crisis and it shall certainly come sometime round the corner!

This is also true with the competition, which has perhaps not fallen into a permanent winter sleep and waits till the spring looks in with still more orders. This attitude is dangerous for an organization, since it indeed needs some time in order to implement measures for the improvement of the profit situation, which cannot certainly be realized overnight.

The questioning of all the processes should

take place regularly (every year) and the „courage for gap" which is also valid here is decisive to achieve a stronger position in the market.

## IS EVERYTHING REALLY SO IMPORTANT?

The validation process includes above all being able to question everything. Naturally also the management is caught in a certain problem having to make unpleasant decisions. Since a long time, rather since a number of years, they have worked together with the colleagues. The conflicts thus stand clearly on the decision-making path, however let us look at it in a simple manner. If the undertaking has to survive further in the market, adjustments must be made repeatedly. Rigid and preserving systems shall die out like the dinosaurs. The economic history can list a number of cases in this respect. Even market leaders were or are not exempted from this. Examples like the undertaking EUMIG just to name an example have now had not only to pay their price for this attitude, but these also simply once leading undertakings do not exist anymore. EUMIG reported bankruptcy in 1982. The brand was sold.

To introduce new ways or to leave behind old established processes, and if it is sensible, to throw them out, i.e. sell them to outsiders, is no shame and resignation from the market.

Managers, who want to be evaluated according to number of employees and turnover, evaluate their personal sensitivities. The profit and the success of e undertaking, should stand in foreground

After the competence onion was worked out, one can begin with the questioning. The core process and the supporting processes which are important in order to realize the core process, should remain, all the other processes should be sold out.

## SIMPLIFY YOUR LIFE

If the manager has the profit of the undertaking before his eyes and if he has outsourced the non-core processes, the manager will learn very fast that with the outsourcing also a few problems stand on the agenda. Many problems occur not in the core process, many problems occur in the support or secondary processes and also demand their resources. Resources, which however perhaps cannot work on the core processes and thus mutate from productive employee to non-productive employee. The employees cause expenses and costs, which do not support the core business to become more economical.

Are these problems and the costs incurred through them sensible for the undertaking? Or is it perhaps better to deposit these problems elsewhere. In case of undertakings, which perhaps title exactly these activities as their core process and are placed substantially better to take over these tasks profitably. A classic example is IT. These main processes could be competences, which can be outsourced. Does it really need in a production unit an own department, which Client Services offers? In case of small undertakings, also the bookkeeping or personnel accounts may be questioned. In periods, where a network makes the data omnipresent, und votes can be comfortably implemented via video conferencing calls, this consideration is really appropriate. The costs for this have substantially improved thanks to the technology and possibilities, as well as the costs for these services, caused by the competition in the free market.

With a small difference that then the resources must not be supported by the own company. Similarly, no absentees and other personnel topics.

## LET YOURSELF BE HELPED!

In case of old established undertakings often a kind of blindness for the undertaking is to be observed. This is nothing reprehensible, even though a countermeasure against this is adopted in order to defuse the situation.

The proverb, you cannot see the forest because of the trees, has a justification. In order to act against this, the following measures can be undertaken.

- Internal Audits /Workshops
- Consulting an external specialist

## Internal Audits / Workshops:

Internal Audits or strategy workshops can be an enrichment of the point of view, in so far as the undertaking has several locations and in other areas not only old, experienced employees carry out their work. This is not supposed to mean that old, experienced employees do not bring in additional value into the undertaking. On the contrary, their knowledge is sought and recognized. Far more important is the fact that these employees have not seen since years or decades any other production environment or experienced it. So they have bathed only in their own „juice", to use a metaphor here.

## Consulting an external specialist:

This is increasingly being done, however, even now many decision makers have concerns to fetch an external specialist. The reason for this lies in the opening up of all data and strategies, and on the other hand before the cost wave, which an undertaking encounters, when the thoughts go in the direction of a large consultancy company.

Both concerns are valid reasons. In the first point, about disclosure, a basic safety can be created by means of contracts. For the second point, it need not always be a large consultancy company. There is also an alternative for this. That of the Interim Manager, who, with his experience from other mandates and his outside view can contribute a considerable additional value. The difference between a consultancy company and an Interim Manager is that a good and renowned Interim Manager from a line function can also lead the implementation. He takes over thus responsibility in the modification process and does not simply throw colorful presentations on the wall, which were already sold a number of times.

An Interim Manager, made available by a renowned „Provider house", is also connected with costs, however, the practical connection and the speed for implementation are substantially higher.

## QUESTIONNAIRE:

- Why one must work continuously on the topics / Problems?

- What is the highest objective of every corporation?

- Which alternative can be referred to as support?

- Why is an external view profitable?

- What distinguishes a consultancy company from an Interim Manager / Leader?

5 rules of operative optimization

## DEFINE ROLES & RESPONSIBILITIES

The definition of roles and responsibilities is an important one, especially since the definition regulates all functions in the undertaking and thus also the efficiency.

In the growth of an undertaking, often positions and leadership responsibilities are given to employees, who are already since long in the undertaking or who represent the best experts. The concerned employees indeed feel honored and thankful for the better wages, however, the management must ask itself, whether this employee is really the first choice for this position and whether it would not have been better to find someone internally as well as externally, who happily takes over the responsibility of leadership. Because in many instances, due to the above-mentioned reasons, the new position is attractive. However, only for a short period, because in the new role, many responsibilities come to the employee, which have nothing to do with the expert knowledge, and unpleasant subjects come on the table for the employee. It is not important, whether this involves interdisciplinary or economic subjects. At first as colleague, then as manager, because, over a long period the employee shall not present himself as management, except when he prepares himself for the role and was actively involved in the decision.

Under a role & responsibility regulation there is more than only the placement of individual employees on certain positions, or the creation of a job profile. The roles and responsibilities define all functions of the respective employee and also rule the responsibilities, which the individual employee has to assume in the given level.

## CHANGE OF ORGANIZATION

After the outsourcing of the non-sustainable processes and competences was competed, perhaps other or lightly modified positions and hierarchies' result. The organization chart must eventually be matched, and employees must be transferred from one position into another position. What however all positions and hierarchies have in common, is the fact that these must be clearly defined in order to ensure the desired effect of efficient achievement of the objective.

The changes in organization chart often cause insecurity in the employees. Therefore, it is the more important to communicate here clearly and unequivocally where the trip goes on one hand and on the other hand, which effects these changes shall have on the respective individual case. A very frequent error is to change the organization chart in installments. For the employees during every change the safety thought acquires a new high value and thus blocks the performance of the respective employee.

Counteracting this, the organization chart can at once be changed, however, it must be prepared according to general staff. Departments like the personnel department and the managers of the core process area as well as the managers of individual affected areas must be involved in this.

Should an agile form of organization be selected, then special value and focus must be placed on the middle management, since the largest changes shall take place there. Similarly, it is important and a pre-requisite that all the positions and levels show a clear role description and responsibility regulation, and the relevant employees receive the capability, before results can be demanded from them.

Ability before achieving the target, so that results can be implemented sustainably.

## WHO PLAYS WHICH INSTRUMENT?

For preparing the awarding of different positions in the new organization structure, an evaluation of the competences of each individual employee should be carried out. Often capabilities are discovered in individual employees, which were previously not really known, or were not promoted by others. These capabilities could really help the organization to reach the objectives more efficiently. For analysis of the capabilities of the organization a qualification and flexibility matrix are recommended, to work out together with the employees and the managers.

## The qualification matrix

The qualification matrix serves to document the training of each individual employee. Similarly, the degree of knowledge is visibly represented in the form of a gradation. During this it is not significant, whether this is implemented with a list or in a computer system. It is only important that this is done and thus a qualification/capability matrix about many a decision about who shall be deployed where can be implemented more objectively.

## The Flexibility matrix

The flexibility matrix deals with the lineup and documentation, as to which work processes of the individual employees are in which experience level. Also, here it does not matter, where this is implemented, so long as it takes place.

## CLEARNESS BRINGS PERFORMANCE

One of the greatest blockades of the employee output is the thought about safety. This shapes up, when employees do not know where the undertaking train is travelling, where the seat for the employee is, or / and not in Change Process is connected. False or too little communication represents the main reasons for failure. With the defined roles and responsibilities of each individual employee, the individual employee knows, what the organization expects from him and in the ideal case makes available to him also the ability in the form of trainings and schoolings. Through the structure of the roles and responsibilities the employee knows himself and discovers himself in the organization.

With this clarity the employee can align his performance and his deployment clearly and thus he is a profit-contributing employee in the undertaking.

In a productive organization the following functional areas are referred to as structure:

- Work safety and environment
- Quality
- Productivity
- Costs
- Stocks &
- Organization development

In this structure the employees discover themselves, since these areas do not represent new areas and are partly familiar.

## THE BRAKE OF SAFETY CONSIDERATIONS

Safety consideration is not a thing, which the employee cannot deal with, in so far as the reasons of the safety considerations do not have the upper hand. As soon as the daily output of the employee is negatively impaired, counteraction must be taken from the management side. As already mentioned in a previous chapter, uncertainties are caused by the missing integration or the poor communication. The environment, where the individual employee can motivate himself continuously, is deformed and in the worst case destroyed. The performance follows in the footsteps of motivation and just breaks away. The performance of the individual is not the only thing to suffer. Much rather this mood spreads around and infects other employees. The reversal to a positive direction is not achievable in a comparable period and the expenses are considerably higher than in the motivated condition.

Safety consideration in the most negative form comes to light, when the work safety is impaired. When an employee is afraid about coming back home with the same health condition, as when he came to work,

then the work performance shall sink in the abyss of wastage.

## QUESTIONNAIRE:

- What are the roles and responsibilities?

- What is that one should pay attention to during change in organization?

- What is a qualification matrix?

- Why is clarity in every function so important?

- What is safety consideration?

- When does safety consideration become a risk?

## ABBREVIATIONS / LEGEND:

| | |
|---|---|
| BPD | Business Plan Deployment |
| EDMI | Entscheidung, Durchführung, Mitwirkung,Information (Decision, execution, cooperation, information) |
| FTQ | First TimeQuality |
| GAE | Total plant efficiency |
| HR | Human Resources |
| IT | Information Technology |
| KPI | Key Performance Indicator |
| KVP | Continuous improvement process |
| ME | Manufacturing Engineering |
| NA | Not Available |
| PDCA | Plan Do Check Act |
| PKB | Problem communication sheet |
| QM | Quality Management |
| RASI | Responsible Action Support Information |
| TIC | Team Info Center |
| TPM | Total Productive Maintenance |
| Shopfloor | Work area in Production |

**Further Publication:**

5 Regeln der Produktion
ISBN 978-3-8482-2634-4

Kommunikation in der Produktion
ISBN 978-3-8482-5126-1

Rollen & Verantwortlichkeiten in der
Produktion
ISBN 978-3-7322-5290-9

5 rules of production
ISBN 978-3-7357-3675-8

Communication in the production
ISBN 978-3-7347-2963-8

Das Werker Entwicklungs- Programm „WEP"
ISBN 978-3-7494-8058-6

5 Fragen an den Interim Manager
ISBN 978-3-7519-5860-8

5 questions about interim management
ISBN 978-3-7386-4639-9

5 Regeln der operativen Optimierung
ISBN: 9783752685794

Potentiale nutzen!
ISBN: 9783752640199